HAL•LEONARD
INSTRUMENTAL
PLAY-ALONG

Disney
Hannah Montana

HOW TO USE THE CD ACCOMPANIMENT:
THE CD IS PLAYABLE ON ANY CD PLAYER. FOR PC AND
MAC USERS, THE CD IS ENHANCED SO YOU CAN ADJUST
THE RECORDING TO ANY TEMPO WITHOUT CHANGING PITCH.

A MELODY CUE APPEARS ON THE RIGHT CHANNEL ONLY. IF YOUR
CD PLAYER HAS A BALANCE ADJUSTMENT, YOU CAN ADJUST THE
VOLUME OF THE MELODY BY TURNING DOWN THE RIGHT CHANNEL.

Disney characters and artwork © Disney Enterprises, Inc.

ISBN 978-1-4234-6103-6

Walt Disney Music Company
Wonderland Music Company, Inc.

DISTRIBUTED BY

HAL•LEONARD®
CORPORATION

7777 W. BLUEMOUND RD. P.O. BOX 13819 MILWAUKEE, WI 53213

In Australia Contact:
Hal Leonard Australia Pty. Ltd.
4 Lentara Court
Cheltenham, Victoria, 3192 Australia
Email: ausadmin@halleonard.com.au

Visit Hal Leonard Online at
www.halleonard.com

◆ BEST OF BOTH WORLDS

TRUMPET

Words and Music by MATTHEW GERRARD
and ROBBIE NEVIL

5

6

♦② BIGGER THAN US

TRUMPET

Words and Music by TIM JAMES
and ANTONINA ARMATO

◆❸ FIND YOURSELF IN YOU

Words and Music by MATTHEW GERRARD,
AMBER HEZLEP, JULIA ROSS
and SARAH ROSS

TRUMPET

◆ I GOT NERVE

Words and Music by JEANNIE LURIE,
KEN HAUPTMAN and ARUNA ABRAMS

TRUMPET

Up-tempo Rock

◆5 I LEARNED FROM YOU

Words and Music by MATTHEW GERRARD
and STEVE DIAMOND

TRUMPET

◆ JUST LIKE YOU

TRUMPET

Words and Music by ANDREW DODD
and ADAM WATTS

❼ LIFE'S WHAT YOU MAKE IT

Words and Music by MATTHEW GERRARD
and ROBBIE NEVIL

TRUMPET

◆8 NOBODY'S PERFECT

TRUMPET

Words and Music by MATTHEW GERRARD
and ROBBIE NEVIL

◆ OLD BLUE JEANS

Words and Music by MICHAEL BRADFORD
and PAM SHEYNE

TRUMPET

🔟 PUMPIN' UP THE PARTY

TRUMPET

Words and Music by
JAMIE HOUSTON

Funky Pop

◈ ONE IN A MILLION

TRUMPET

Words and Music by TOBY GAD
and NEGIN DJAFARI

THE OTHER SIDE OF ME

TRUMPET

Words and Music by MATTHEW GERRARD,
ROBBIE NEVIL and JAY LANDERS

⑬ ROCK STAR

Words and Music by JEANNIE LURIE,
ARIS ARCHONTIS and CHEN NEEMAN

TRUMPET

◆ 14 WE GOT THE PARTY

Words and Music by
KARA DioGUARDI

TRUMPET

15 TRUE FRIEND

Words and Music by
JEANNIE LURIE

TRUMPET

Moderate Pop